Ceremonies and Celebrations
FEASTS AND FASTING

KERENA MARCHANT

HODDER
Wayland

an imprint of Hodder Children's Books

Ceremonies and Celebrations

FEASTS AND FASTING

Other titles in this series are:

BIRTHS • WEDDINGS • GROWING UP
LIFE'S END • PILGRIMAGES AND JOURNEYS

Produced for Hodder Wayland by
Roger Coote Publishing
Gissing's Farm, Fressingfield
Suffolk IP21 5SH, UK

Published in Great Britain in 2000 by Hodder Wayland, an imprint of
Hodder Children's Books

© Hodder Wayland 2000

Editor: Alex Edmonds
Designer: Tim Mayer

Consultants:

Khadijah Knight is a teacher and consultant on multicultural education
and Islam. She is also the author of several children's books about Islam.

Marcus Braybrooke is a parish priest and lecturer and writer on inter-
faith relations. He is joint President of the World Congress of Faiths.

Kanwaljit Kaur-Singh is a local authority inspector for education.
She has written many books on the Sikh tradition and appears on
television regularly.

Sharon Barron regularly visits schools to talk to children about Judaism.
She has written two books about Judaism for Hodder Wayland.

Meg St. Pierre is the Director of the Clear Vision Trust, a charitable
trust that aims to inform and educate about the teachings of Buddha.

VP Hemant Kanitkar is a retired teacher and author of many books
on Hinduism.

The right of Kerena Marchant to be identified as the author of this
Work has been asserted by her in accordance with the Copyright,
Designs and Patents Act 1988.

Picture acknowledgements
Circa Picture Library 6, 18 (William Holtby); Hutchison Library
front cover centre right (Nigel Howard), 1 (Nigel Howard), 8 (Nigel
Howard), 21 (Juliet Highet), 26 (Patricio Goycoolea), 27 (Liba
Taylor), 29 (Nigel Howard); Panos Pictures 28 (Daniel O'Leary);
Peter Sanders *front cover* top left, 4, 14, 17; Tony Stone Images *front
cover* top right (Leland Bobbe); Trip *front cover* bottom left (H
Rogers), 5 (H Rogers), 7 (H Rogers), 9 (H Rogers), 10 (S Shapiro),
11 (H Rogers), 12 (A Tovy), 13 (A Tovy), 15 (C Rennie), 16 (H
Rogers), 19 (H Rogers), 20 (Dinodia), 22 (H Rogers), 23 (H Rogers),
24 (H Rogers), 25 (B Dhanjal).

A Catalogue record for this book is available from the
British Library.
ISBN 0 7502 2804 0

Printed and bound in Italy by G Canale & C. S.p.A. Turin, Italy

Hodder Children's Books
a division of Hodder Headline Limited
338 Euston Road, London NW1 3BH

CONTENTS

Food and Faith

Food and drink are two of the most important things in our lives. Without food and drink we would die. How people feel about food and drink tells us a lot about their beliefs, their relationship with other people and with nature. They might choose to keep well and healthy by eating all the right things. They could believe that killing animals, birds and fish is wrong and not eat meat.

People from many religions eat special food on important religious days because it reminds them of God or their beliefs. At times they might go without food so that they can think more about God and people less well off than themselves. They might want to share a special occasion with friends or family over a meal.

▲ *Hindu* sadhus *or holy men fast because they believe that depriving their body of food makes their faith stronger.*

When to feast

Feasts are a time of celebration when people remember special times, such as the birth of a religious leader or an important historical event. Many religions have special food that is eaten at feasts that helps people remember the events behind the celebration. A feast is often a holiday and a time for friends and family to get together. On these occasions the food is often enough to feed large numbers or is more expensive than the food that would normally be eaten. Some religions don't encourage their followers to eat expensive food, even at feasts, mindful that food can divide the rich and the poor.

When to fast

Different religions fast for different reasons. Sometimes people fast because they believe that suffering makes them closer to God, perhaps before making a new promise or before starting a new way of life. Fasting is believed to concentrate the mind on holy thoughts. There are some religions, such as Sikhism and Buddhism, that don't encourage fasting because they do not believe it helps deepen religious strength.

Food laws

Religions have different rules about what you can eat and drink. Some Jewish people only eat and drink kosher food which is prepared in a special way according to the laws of Judaism, whereas most Christians can eat and drink anything. A lot of people don't eat meat at all, such as some Hindus, Buddhists or Sikhs. Muslims eat halal meat, which comes from animals that are killed in a special way. Hindus and Buddhists don't eat meat because they believe that life is sacred. Sikhs avoid any food that they feel 'harms the body or provokes evil thoughts'. This means that some Sikhs choose not to drink alcohol.

▲ *A Sikh vegetarian meal of sag paneer (spinach and cheese), dhal (lentils), rice, roti (bread) and raita (yoghurt and cucumber).*

The Christian Tradition

Lent and Easter

Lent is the period of 40 weekdays before Easter. It is a time when Christians think more about how they live their lives and try to strengthen their faith. It is also a time to prepare for Easter, when they remember the death and resurrection (raising from the dead) of Jesus Christ. Christians all over the world approach Lent in different ways. Some might try to make their faith stronger by giving up a favourite food, such as chocolate, and not giving in to temptation. Others might give up all dairy products. The Orthodox Church keeps Lent more strictly and people give up both meat and diary products. Some Christians will attend Lenten Bible studies to look deeper into their faith and their personal lives and learn how to become better Christians.

◀ Making pancakes on Shrove Tuesday, the day before the start of Lent. Pancakes are made from milk, eggs and flour.

Shrove Tuesday is the day before Lent and traditionally Christians make pancakes. This comes from an old tradition where fatty food in the house had to be used up before the fasting period of Lent began. Lent officially begins on Ash Wednesday. The name comes from the fact that priests used to mark the forehead of Christians with ashes, to show that they are totally dependent on God, and as worthless as ashes without him.

Sacred text

This text talks about fasting and how Christians should not fast for glory. Many men would paint their faces to show that they were fasting. Jesus tells his disciples to clean their faces and keep their fasting secret.

'When you fast, do not look sombre as the hypocrites do, for they disfigure their faces to show men they are fasting. I tell you the truth, they have received their reward in full. But when you fast, put oil on your head and wash your face, so that it will not be obvious to men that you are fasting, but only to your Father, who is unseen; and your Father, who sees what is done in secret, will reward you.'

The Bible: Matthew 6:1—6

◄ On Good Friday in Greece religious icons are decorated and paraded round the streets.

▲ *In the Greek Orthodox tradition, the first day of Lent is called Clean Monday because no meat or animal products can be eaten. Villagers share a special meal to celebrate this day.*

Easter Sunday

Easter Sunday, two days after Good Friday, is when Christ rose from the dead. It is a very important day in the Christian calendar and a day of celebration and feasting. Easter feasts vary around the world, though most of the food eaten is symbolic. Lamb is traditionally eaten because the last meal that Jesus ate before his death was a Jewish Passover meal of lamb. The richest Easter feasts are in the Orthodox tradition where all the foods forbidden during Lent are eaten on Easter Day.

Katiyah's story

'My name is Katiyah and I'm 12 years old. My family are Greek Orthodox. Easter Sunday begins at midnight when the priest comes out of church carrying a candle and announces that Christ has risen. After the service we go home for a meal of Easter eggs. These are eggs that are dyed red. Later that day our family gathers to swap Easter eggs and eat cakes and breads. In the evening we eat a meal of lamb stuffed with almonds and raisins.'

The Last Supper

Communion is a regular part of the Christian church service that reminds Christians of the last meal that Christ shared with his disciples. Bread and wine are given to the whole congregation. Sometimes special wafers are used or a loaf of bread is cut up. The wine is drunk from a large goblet called a chalice. In some churches non-alcoholic grape juice may be drunk in place of wine. To many Christians this ritual is a regular way of remembering Christ.

◄ Children look at traditional and modern Easter eggs and cakes. The red eggs are coloured with onion dye. The round cake is a simnel cake which is traditionally eaten at Easter.

The Jewish Tradition

Yom Kippur

Yom Kippur is the Day of Atonement when Jews believe that they are punished for past sins and can pray for the future. It comes ten days after the New Year, *Rosh Hashanah*. The days between *Rosh Hashanah* and *Yom Kippur* are called the Days of Repentance. During this period, Jews think about their relationship with God and ask forgiveness for their sins, so that they can start the year afresh. *Yom Kippur* is a solemn time when Jews feel that they have to show they want forgiveness for their sins by practising self-discipline. They do this by fasting and praying. Jews believe that fasting can make a person more compassionate. The Jewish tradition of compassion is shown in the ritual of sending food – often chicken – to the poor at this time of year.

A family shares a new year feast together at Rosh Hashanah. ▼

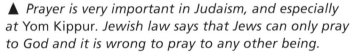

▲ *Prayer is very important in Judaism, and especially at* Yom Kippur. *Jewish law says that Jews can only pray to God and it is wrong to pray to any other being.*

Sacred text

This is one of the prayers that is recited at *Yom Kippur*:

'Take away my shame,
Lift my anxiety,
Absolve me of my sin
And enable me to pray before Thee
With gladness of heart,
To pursue Thy commandments and
Thy Torah
In the joy of holiness.'

Yom Kippur prayer

The day before *Yom Kippur* is a feast day and the meal is a *mitzvah* meal, which is a meal that must be eaten. It should be a happy, festive time in contrast with *Yom Kippur*. Jews light candles for the table and say prayers for dead relations. They wear their best clothes and serve lavish meals, although they tend not to serve spicy or sweet dishes which might make them thirsty or be hard to digest. It is important that everybody prepares for the fast the next day by eating well the day before, so that they can give serious thought to their sins during the fasting period.

Jews fast at *Yom Kippur* because it is commanded that they do in the *Torah*: 'In the seventh month, on the tenth day of the month, you shall afflict your souls,' (*Torah*: Leviticus 16:29). The day of *Yom Kippur* is a day of fasting in order that nothing, not even food preparation, can distract people from attending services at the synagogue. They should be praying and remembering everything they have done wrong in the past year. Only adults who are healthy and fit can fast. It is important to remember every wrongdoing that day so that God can forgive them all. Jews believe that once *Yom Kippur* is over at sunset, it is too late to remember forgotten sins and be forgiven.

Jews visit the Wailing Wall during the fasting period of Yom Kippur. ▼

▲ *A priest blows the shofar to signify the end of the day's prayers.*

Hayyim's story

'My name is Hayyim, I am 12 and I live in Prague in the Czech Republic. At *Yom Kippur* we go straight to the synagogue without eating. Most of the day is spent there. Everybody asks for forgiveness for their sins.

The day in the synagogue comes to an end in the evening when the *shofar*, a musical instrument made from a ram's horn, is blown. It's time to celebrate as all our sins are forgiven. After the service we go home to break our fast with a meal of cold chicken and carrot pudding.'

The Muslim Tradition

Ramadan fast and Id feast

Ramadan is the month during which Muslims fast from before sunrise to sunset. It remembers the time when the Prophet Muhammad (Peace Be Upon Him) received the first revelation of the Qur'an, the Muslim holy book, from the Angel Jibril. The fast is one of the Five Pillars of Islam, the five things that all Muslims must do. They don't think of the hardships of fasting – going without water during the day in hot countries, or in cold countries having no food or hot drinks to keep warm. They only think about the benefits of fasting. Muslims believe that fasting brings you closer to God and helps you to think more about what God wants you to do. Muslims may resolve to improve their behaviour in different ways after the fast and generally try to become better people. *Ramadan* is a time of prayer, and Muslims often have competitions during which they recite the Qur'an to each other for long periods.

Breaking the fast with an iftar meal of dates. ▼

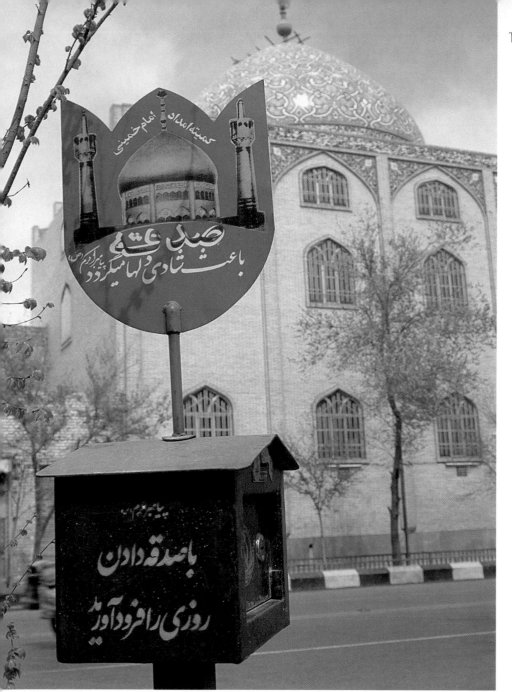

◄ *A zakat or charity box outside a mosque.*

Sacred text

'O company of Muslims, go to the generous God, who gave you the good things and grants the great reward. For God ordered you to pray during the night, so you prayed, ordered you to fast during the day, so you fasted and obeyed your Lord, so now take your reward.'

From the *Sayings of The Prophet Muhammad*

Many Muslims break their fast every evening with a light *iftar* meal of water and dates. Drinking water and eating dates means that the body gets both energy and water after the day's fast. Dates and water are easy to find in many Muslim countries and both rich and poor can eat these. After they have shared this food together, families go to the mosque for the *maghrib*, or sunset prayers. Then they can go home for their main meal together, which is traditionally rice and yoghurt with chicken or meat.

Ramadan is also a time when people think about forgiveness and being generous to others. Muslims give a gift of food or money called *Zakat-ul-Fitr*, to the mosque so that everyone, even the most needy, can feast and celebrate after the *Id* prayers when the fast is broken. The new moon that ends the *Ramadan* fast brings the *Id-ul-Fitr* festivities and feasting. *Id-ul-Fitr* is a celebration of what Muslims have achieved and learnt during the fast. They celebrate having the strength to fast as the Fourth of the Five Pillars of Islam (the five main points of Islamic law) has told them to. *Id-ul-Fitr* is also a time to celebrate the fact that God allowed the Qur'an to be revealed to humans.

Cards to wish everyone a happy Id. *In Islam it is forbidden to draw people, so the children decorate their cards with traditional Islamic patterns and the* Id *moon.* ▼

Ahmed's story

'My name is Ahmed, and I live in Morocco. Tonight is the Night of Power when we remember the night that the Angel Jibril recited the Qur'an to the Prophet Muhammad (pbuh). The Night of Power falls during the month of *Ramadan*. After sunset I have a light *iftar* meal of some water and dates, followed by a bowl of *harira* soup, made from chick peas and other pulses. After dinner I make my way to the mosque, where the Qur'an will be read all night to the beating of a drum.'

Many Muslims prepare for the day by bathing and wearing their best clothes. Often they wear traditional perfumes. Children are given gifts by their families and some women receive presents from their loved ones. The day begins with prayers just after sunrise. At the end of a day of joyful prayers, families gather together for a big meal consisting of rich foods and pastries, cakes and sweets.

After reading the Qur'an in the mosque, the congregation share a meal to break their Ramadan fast. ▶

The Hindu Tradition

Fasting and feasting at Janmashtami

▲ *A Brahmin* priest reads the Hindu scriptures. Holy men like this believe that fasting cleanses the mind and helps them to understand religious texts.

Janmashtami is the Hindu festival that celebrates the birth of Krishna. Very often Indian towns will be colourfully decorated with lights and flowers. Hindus fast at festivals and at other times to show devotion to the Hindu deities (gods). Fasting helps people break free of day-to-day worries and thoughts, so that prayers and meditation can go uninterrupted. Hindus will go to specially decorated Krishna temples at *Janmashtami* to pray.

Sacred text

This sacred text warns Hindus that they will become like a serpent if they don't observe the fast of *Janmashtami*.

'Whether a man or woman, if one neglects to observe the birthday vrata (ceremony) of Lord Krishna, the Krishna Janmashtami – born as a female serpent in a deep forest.'

From the *Bhavishya Purana*

For some people the fast will mean no food at all, and only the odd drink of water. For others it will mean a simple diet of milk, yoghurt, fruit and root vegetables. In the hours leading up to midnight, people will go to the temple and sing sacred songs called *bhajans*. In Hindu temples the statues of the deities are always dressed in clothes and on festive occasions they wear festive clothes.

Statues of Krishna and his wife Radha are dressed in festive clothes at Janmashtami. ▼

◀ At Janmashtami *a human pyramid is formed to recreate the story of how Krishna climbed up to the top of a house to steal some butter.*

When midnight, the hour of Krishna's birth, arrives, a special *arati* ceremony begins. During this ceremony a statue of Krishna as a baby is bathed in milk, honey, ghee, flowers and water, and placed in a crib and rocked. Krishna's favourite food – desserts made from dairy products and sweets – are offered to him. Food like this which is offered to a deity is called *prasad*. Once the food has been offered to Krishna, the rest is shared among the worshippers. The following day there will be festivities. Plays about Krishna will be acted and stories told. Family and friends will share festive meals and give each other sweets.

This statue shows Krishna playing his flute. ▼

Champa's story

'My name is Champa. I live in the USA. The nearest Hindu temple is too far to drive to, so festivals are a family time and are celebrated in the home. Around our house are statues of the Hindu Gods. They are a sign that the deities live in our house and are like members of the family. We have to wash, dress and feed them. Before we eat a meal we make sure the Gods are fed before we sit down to eat.'

The Sikh Tradition

Fasting

Sikhism started in India with beliefs and practices which are different from Islam and Hinduism – the other main religions of India. One of the ways it differed was in fasting. Sikhs believe that your soul will only get close to God if you live a good life and serve God. They believe that fasting does not help you to know what God wants or give any spiritual benefits; it only makes you ill.

One of the most important Sikh *gurus*, Guru Nanak, taught the Sikhs that fasting was not helpful, but good behaviour is, when he said: 'Let good conduct be thy fasting'. Instead of fasting, Sikhs believe that they should celebrate important days in the Sikh calendar by doing *sewa*. This is when they give offerings of money or do good deeds for people in need.

▲ *Making the* langar *meal in the* Guru ka langar *is a social occasion when all members of the community can get together.*

Langar

During Sikh festivities, importance is given to the sharing of food. Everybody, rich and poor, shares in a communal meal called a *langar* which is eaten in the *gurdwara*. This meal is prepared by worshippers in the *gurdwara*, in the *Guru ka langar*, the 'kitchen of the Guru'. In India the meal is served throughout the day, but outside of India the meal is after the service. This meal is a sign of equality because everybody eats a meal that is the same. It is also a sign of traditional Indian hospitality, and friends and family who have travelled a long way to the *gurdwara* have a chance to share a meal together.

Sacred text

'I do not keep the Hindu fast,
nor the Muslim Ramadan
I serve him alone who is my refuge
I serve the one master who is also Allah.
I have broken with the Hindu and the Muslim.
I Believe God can be revealed
by observing commandments, righteous living,
and Guru Nanak's morning prayer.'

Guru Arjan's Hymn

Worshippers at the Golden Temple at Amritsar share a langar *meal. Many would have travelled a long way to visit this temple, which is the centre of the Sikh belief.* ▶

Sikh festivals are known as *gurpurbs*, which means *'gurus' days'*. During the festival to celebrate Guru Nanak's birthday, Sikhs share a communal meal, or *langar*. Guru Nanak was the first Sikh *guru*. On major festivals such as this, *langar* is served over three days. The food has to be vegetarian because Sikhs believe that eating meat is unclean, so there is no meat, fish or even eggs in the dishes. In the Punjab, where Sikhism comes from, shops, offices and *gurdwaras* are beautifully decorated with lights, and candles are lit and put in the windows of houses. Sikhs give their children new clothes to celebrate the Guru's birthday.

During worship at Sikh gurdwaras, prasad *is shared among worshippers to show that everyone is equal.* Prasad *is a mixture of semolina, butter and sugar.* ▼

▲ The Guru Granth Sahib *is taken round Southall, London on a float to celebrate Guru Nanak's birthday.*

Sandeep's story

'My name is Sandeep and I live in Southall, London. I love the festival of Guru Nanak's birthday. Our holy book, the *Guru Granth Sahib*, is read from beginning to end. After the reading, the *Guru Granth Sahib* is taken round Southall on a float. Everybody follows, singing hymns. The procession ends back at the *gurdwara* where there are talks about the life of Guru Nanak. My father listens to the talks broadcast through loud speakers as he helps cook the *langar*. I like the meal after the service as everybody takes part. It's quite a simple meal: dhal, rice, roti and vegetable curry, but what is special is everybody sharing the same meal.'

Sikhs organize processions through the streets with a 'float' that carries the Sikh holy book, the *Guru Granth Sahib*. The float is richly decorated, and as they walk through the streets, the people share out fruit, cakes and sweets. People walk behind the float singing hymns written by Guru Nanak and children play music and dance.

The Buddhist Tradition

The avoidance of greed

Meditation is one of the ways to achieve Enlightenment, rather than fasting. ▼

One of the things that Buddhists seek to avoid is greed, which they believe leads to unhappiness. Many Buddhists are vegetarian because they are committed to not harming any creatures. Modern Buddhists also try to avoid foods that contribute to the destruction of the environment in the way they are grown or harvested. Buddhists all over the world try to find contentment with a simple diet, and avoid exotic foods. The Buddha taught Buddhists to follow the Middle Way. This is a path between self-indulgence and self-torture. So neither fasting nor great feasting is encouraged.

Buddhists believe that food should be taken in moderation. Buddhist nuns and monks are taught that they should eat in moderation, and only at set times. Buddhists believe that greed prevents them from reaching Enlightenment. Buddhist teachings say that life is an endless wheel: people are born, they live, die and are then reborn again and again. Their aim is to achieve Enlightenment and escape from the wheel by behaving well. Buddhists also believe that people do not own their bodies. A person's body belongs to his or her ancestors and future generations, so everyone has a duty to eat healthily and stay fit.

Buddhist monks queue up with their begging bowls to receive food from local people. ▼

Buddhist festivals are always joyful occasions, and people generally go to a temple or monastery to offer food to the monks and listen to a talk about their faith. Most festivals are celebrated by distributing food to the poor in the community. Food is something to be shared, and even in poor places Buddhists will willingly give food to monks and people they feel are more needy than they are.

Sacred text

This text tells Buddhists that they must live sensibly and not give in to temptation.

'Whoever lives only for pleasures, with senses uncontrolled, immoderate in eating, lazy, and weak, will be overthrown … like the wind throws down a weak tree.'

From *The Sayings of the Buddha*

◄ *Monks offer food to volunteers who harvest the monastery crops. The monks, in turn, are fed by local people.*

Guru Rinpoche

Guru Rinpoche's birthday is a time of great festivity in the Buddhist calendar. The festival, which celebrates the founder of Tibetan Buddhism's birthday, is a time for meditation and celebration. In northern India, this festival is celebrated in a grand way. Villagers travel for days to the nearest monastery. This part of India is very poor and villagers carry small bags of rice and pulses to eat on their journey. They also bring offerings of barley and grain for the monks they intend to visit at the monastery. Buddhists believe that the monks, who depend entirely on the food offerings from visitors to the temple, help them to learn generosity.

Joanne's story

'I live in Paris with my family. For Guru Rinpoche's birthday this year we went to the monastery first. My mum and dad and I offered flowers and fruit to the statue of the Buddha. After we had listened to some of the Buddha's teachings and meditated, we went to the park where there is a huge statue of the Buddha. There were lots of other Buddhists there and we had a party in the park. Everybody brought lots of food that they'd made and we shared it. My brother and I made lots of new friends and played in the park until it was very late.'

Once at the monastery, everybody offers the food to the Buddha, a sign that the person is offering up all his or her worldly desires and is open to meditation. Meditation takes place in front of the statue of the Buddha and everybody chants mantras. Buddhists hope that this meditation will help them to become kind and wise and more like the Buddha.

When meditation is over, the food that was offered is shared. In India or Tibet, this meal is simple and may include rice, barley, pulses and yak (a Tibetan ox) milk. Many people live in remote areas of Asia and festivals are often their only chance to meet their family and friends and share a meal with them.

Western Buddhists prepare a meal to share at Guru Rinpoche's birthday celebrations. ▼

GLOSSARY

Angel Jibril the Angel who visited the Prophet Muhammad (pbuh) on several occasions. In the Christian tradition he is known as Gabriel.

arati a Hindu ceremony that involves making offers of gifts of incense, food and clothes to deities.

deities gods or goddesses.

Five Pillars of Islam the religious and moral duties of a Muslim.

gurdwara a Sikh temple.

guru (Sikh) one of the 10 Sikh human teacher-saints.

(Buddhist) a name given to a Buddhist teacher who is enlightened.

Guru Granth Sahib the Sikh holy book.

Guru Nanak the founder of Sikhism.

Guru Rinpoche the founder of Tibetan Buddhism.

halal food which Muslims are allowed to eat.

icons paintings of Christ, Mary and other Christian saints in Orthodox churches.

iftar meal the meal that breaks the Ramadan fast.

kapel a skull cap worn by Jewish men.

Krishna the Hindu god Vishnu became Krishna when he came to Earth to overcome evil.

kosher food which is specially prepared in accordance with the laws of Judaism.

langar a shared meal that is eaten in a Sikh *gurdwara*.

mantra mantras are chants used by some Buddhists. They are phrases that are repeated many times. Chanting is thought to help people concentrate on one thing and to help meditation.

meditation Buddhists meditate to remove bad thoughts from their minds. They do this in different ways – by concentrating on an image or a sound or by thinking good thoughts.

mitzvah meal a religious meal that Jewish people are supposed to eat before a ceremony or special occasion.

Orthodox Church the Christian Church in Eastern European and North African countries. This church follows the earliest traditions of the Christian Church.

Passover the Jewish festival of Spring.

Peace Be Upon Him (pbuh) the standard phrase that is repeated after the name of a prophet as a mark of respect.

Qur'an the Muslim holy book.

vegetarian a person who does not eat meat or fish.

Zakat-ul-Fitr the giving of charity in Islam. This is one of the Five Pillars of Islam and all Muslims must do this to equalise wealth.

FURTHER INFORMATION

Books

Looking at Judaism: Special Occasions by Sharon Barron, Wayland, 1998.
Easter by Catherine Chambers, Lion, 1998.
Religions Through Festivals: Buddhism by Peter and Holly Connolly, Longman, 1989.
Hinduism by Dilip Kadodwala, Wayland, 1995.
Celebrate Hindu Festivals by Dilip Kadodwala and Paul Gateshill, Heinemann, 1995.
Islam by Khadijah Knight, Wayland, 1995.
Sikhism by Kanwaljit Kaur-Singh, Wayland, 1995.
Islamic Festivals by Khadijah Knight, Heinemann, 1995.
Id-ul-Fitr by Kerena Marchant, Wayland, 1995.
Feasting for Festivals by Jan Wilson, Lion, 1990.

Websites

http://www.jewishnet.net – A comprehensive Judaic resource.
http://www.sparksmag.com – An electronic magazine for Jewish youth, ages 9–13, with articles, interviews, polls and chat.

http://www.christianity.net/ – An extensive guide with stories, a church locator, and a database of over 9,000 Christian sites.

http://www.islam.org – IslamiCity in Cyberspace. An attractive site that explains about Islam and has a virtual mosque tour and a kids' page (http://www.islam.org/KidsCorner/Default.htm).

http://www.hindunet.org – The Hindu Universe. This web site features a Hindu calendar, a glossary of terms and information on Hindu arts, customs, worship and scripture. Links to other Hindu resources are also included.

http://india.indiagov.org/culture/religion/hinduism.htm – Discover India. Maintained by the Indian government's ministry of external affairs this site gives information on Hindu beliefs and festivals.

http://www.sikhs.org/ – An extensive range of topics, from teachings to ceremonies and festivals. Includes translated scriptures and contemporary articles.

education@clear-vision.org – The web site for the Clear Vision Trust, a project that provides Buddhist resources.

INDEX

All the numbers in **bold** refer to photographs